Terri;

It was such a pleasure to meet
and talk with you and your wonderful
husband. May God continue to
bless you and your entire family.

The

Power Of

Marketing

YOU

Praise for Cornelius D. Jones's
The Power of Marketing You

"GREAT READ."
-Teresa Moss
"EXCELLENT CONCEPT."
-Harriet Fry Education Consultant
"VERY WELL THOUGHT OUT!
-Keyana Brunner

"A must read for anyone who seeks a step-by-step approach guide for catching the attention of others, maintaining the connection and delivering clear as well as effective messages within any size group setting."
-Dr. Adrianne Morton Georgian Court University

"A good read, as a prior Navy man and a recruiter I could definitely relate to your story."
-James Owens USN SCPO (ret)
"Clear, detailed, potential good read."
-Michael Ziegler Investment Advisor

"After reading this I immediately put it into practice."

-Antonio Arlington Financial Advisor

"Pretty straightforward and flows well."

- *Tyrone Bledsoe, PhD Founder SAAB*

"Creatively poignant read that will affect individuals personally and professionally to succeed on all levels of self-enrichment."

- *Dr. Ernest E. Cutler, EdD, USN (ret)*

C.D. Jones Books

Published by Lulu Publishing Inc.

2014 edition: Janice Bradley editor

Publication date 7/23/2014

ISBN: 978-1-312-32162-5

Manufactured in the United States of America

Library of Congress Cataloging - in - Publication Data

Jones, Cornelius D

The Power of Marketing You: Talking your way to success / Cornelius Jones.
p.cm. www.corneliusdjones.org

Our mission is to create and distribute inspirational products offering exceptional value and encouragement to the masses.

Table of Contents

ACKNOWLEDGMENTS

TO THE FIRST EDITION

THE PEOPLE LISTED BELOW all commented on CHAPTERs, suggested sources, corrected my mistakes, or provided other moral or material aid. There were so many, who offered encouragement, provided feedback and supported my vision on this project. I thank you very much. They are: Antonio Arlington, Brandon Ash, Ernest Cutler, Harriet Fry, Keyana Brunner, Jenneta Parker, James Owens, David Beck, Thomas Hardy Jr., Michael Ziegler, Tyrone Bledsoe, Teresa Moss, Colon Ragston, Mark Ross, Victoria Westfield, Vivica Parker, and especially my wonderful editor, Janice Bradley, who provided consistent encouragement and intelligent criticism. It is such a blessing to have people that I can count on to give me the truth when I need to hear it the most.

There is no shortage of people that I would like to acknowledge and thank, there are so many instrumental figures in my life that are worthy of being mentioned. I'm just grateful to have all of you as friends.

Introduction

No matter what field you work in, you need to be able to market yourself. Nothing reveals more about who you are than what you say about yourself. However, if you really want people to stand up and take notice then this is the book for you.

Using real-life anecdotes from my own life experiences, I present tools to help you develop the basic skills and winning character traits that people will not only notice; they will remember. My book will show you how to:

- Boost your self-worth and demonstrate it to others

- Identify your most dynamic personal qualities

- Become a master of the fine art of listening and use it to get ahead on your job and in life.

- Talk with anyone

- Be universally liked

- Influence and persuade others.

The ability to sell requires the desire and comprehension to market. It is unreasonable to believe that products become household names without a pitchman. The pitchman's primary responsibility is to sell the idea of the product to companies seeking to boost revenue sales with the latest and greatest on the market. Once the company agrees to carry the item, they then invest in all-out blitz advertisement campaigns to get that product from the stores selves to the homes of potential consumers.

You are your own product. What you have to offer potential employers is invaluable and it is up to you to advertise that correctly the first time around. Without solid marketing and presentation of your attributes you will never be afforded the opportunity to showcase your skills to the employer. Here is what I want to do for you; I want to teach you the art of selling and marketing yourself.

Pay close attention to these words: marketing and selling yourself. Individually, these words carry a certain weight; however, when put them together they present something great – the ability to transform your life. Advertising, marketing, presenting, and selling equals revenue. This is the cornerstone of any company's financial stability. Your ingredient words are ambition, work ethic, determination, and skills/qualifications equals success. This is the cornerstone of the American dream.

Catching the attention of others isn't always the easiest thing to do unless you are willing to wear a big colorful sign or jump up and down while shouting "Hey, here I am look at me!" Even if this is your method of choice it does not mean that you will receive the kind of attention that you wish.

Have you ever stopped to think, why do rich and famous people have a publicist and just what does a publicist do? Publicists and public relations personnel are hired primarily to build and boost the images of their clients to make them more likeable which makes them more marketable.

Many people who have publicists lack the communication skills to win others over on their own merit without the help of others. Well, we all aren't rich; and most of us can't afford to pay tens of thousands of dollars to some firm or person to paint the perfect picture of who we are to potential employers or important circles of people. That's where this book comes in.

CHAPTER 1

Know Your Product

Hi, my name is Cornelius Jones. I have been blessed with the remarkable gift of salesmanship. I want to share that gift with you and show you how you can change everything in your life by being able to market yourself properly. This chapter is not designed to convince you how great I am; rather it is to help you understand the importance of knowing yourself as the product.

Your outerwear, which simply means the way that you carry yourself, is the face of your package. No one buys things that are dirty, rundown, sloppy, or unattractive unless they are into the business of collecting junk. Most people are only interested in purchasing or learning more about things that are well packaged, attractive and neatly organized. You are the product; your character, talents, and abilities make up the content of your product. You must know how to advertise *you* well so that a prospect becomes a buyer without a second thought.

In the past I've found success in selling shoes, cars, organizations, jobs, and even myself through the form of ideas and the personal strategies that I've implemented to help me live a more fulfilling and productive life. For the last 4 years, I have been able to sell countless copies of my books without the help of managers, advertisement companies or a literary agent. I have established a respectable name for myself as an entrepreneur through the art of self-advertisement and marketing everything to which I could attach my name to give me an advantage in an industry filled with competition.

Maximizing social media, the internet, and my personal website, I have been able to eliminate any overhead and continue to generate interest while increasing my net profits by nearly 90%.

I have learned to combine my skills as a public speaker, thought leader, and counselor, as well as my experience as a top recruiter for one of the world's largest organizations into a formula for success.

In this chapter you will learn why and how presenting yourself with a winning attitude can determine your latitude in life. Your attitude determines how high in life you go; you may as well have a good attitude if you expect to have a good shot at succeeding.

This is not an infomercial with a paid actor or actress promising you false results. This book is written by someone just like you, who decided to take my own expectations and turn them into experience. I want to help you develop yourself in ways that you've never thought of before by showing you how to discover your untapped potential below the surface.

Everyone has the ability to go as far in life as their heart desires. The challenge for most of us is that we have yet to discover exactly how far we want to go. One reason for this is most people live their entire lives under a ceiling. This prevents them from maximizing the opportunities we are presented with to reach for the sky and succeed.

Let me explain. If you stand in a room of any building and look up, you will likely see a ceiling of some sort. That ceiling prevents your eyes from seeing anything beyond that point. Let's use that ceiling as your potential of growth or the opportunity to progress in your personal and professional life. As long as you remain under that ceiling you will believe that you can only rise as high as it goes. On the other hand, if you step outside of that building and then look up you quickly realize that there are no limits to how far up you can see or ultimately go in life. Master the art of removing yourself from under the ceiling. Then you will be better equipped to realize your full potential and market yourself accordingly.

Reaching our full potential may require someone else creating an opportunity for us at times. There is an old saying in business that goes something like this, "It's not what you know, it's who you know." If you are still one of the few people in the world who do not believe this statement to be true, I suggest that you open your eyes my friend and take a closer look at life. People are not always put in positions because they are the most qualified but rather because of the intervention of influence.

Here is what normally happens. Someone who knows a key decision-maker does a favor for a third party – a friend, colleague, relative or company. This someone uses their influence with the decision-maker on behalf of the third party that results in the award of a bid, or contract, job, or great promotion. The person in the position of authority gives something of value without really knowing whether or not the third party merits this special attention. This is a form of marketing. Why? Because the person with influence had to present (market) the *value* of the third party_to the person in position to say yes in order for the transaction to be successful.

The Art of Salesmanship

In only a 3-year period, I was directly responsible for helping to recruit nearly 130 people to the Armed Services. I averaged 3.6 new contacts (recruits) per month during one of the Armed Forces most difficult recruiting environments in history partially due to the economy and military budget cuts. This number may not seem like a big deal to you but when you consider the national recruiting average is 1 person a month per recruiter, my accomplishment takes on a new perspective.

Someone reading this may assume that it should have been easy in a down economy to find people to join the military but I can tell you the military's standards do not change in response to shifts in the economy. I will lay out a road map from where I started so that you may have a better understanding of the journey I've traveled as a natural salesperson.

As a boy, my mind often raced with all the things I wanted to do once I grew up, but none stood out more than joining the U.S military. I was always fascinated with great leaders throughout history and their contributions to the nation. They all seemed to possess one special trait. This was the ability to continue to perform under extreme pressure.

In addition to this, they had strong powers of persuasion; enough to convince their followers to take huge risks, despite the probability of great physical harm, for a greater cause. It takes a remarkable amount of salesmanship to impart a willingness in others to fight for the ideals of someone or something else – in this case, our nation.

Serving in the military on some level was an ambition I needed to fulfill as a stepping stone to where I was headed. After a close look at all of the service branches, I was finally ready to make my decision...my branch of choice was the United States Navy. There was just something intriguing about the Navy that made it stand out from the other service branches. Maybe it was partially because of the respect I had for the legacy of renowned leaders and movers and shakers of American history. They had once served in the world's strongest Navy; and I too wanted to be part of it.

In October of 2001, I went to the local recruiting office at the Gwinnet Place Mall located in Gwinnet County, Georgia. I was on a mission. I entered the office with only one thing on my mind; and that was to get the military to pay for my college education. I called in advance to set an appointment with one of the recruiters. I can't recall the recruiter's name but I can recall the awful job he did trying to sell me on the organization. He was like a desperate used car salesman looking to sell the worst lemon on the lot to the first vulnerable customer in the door. I had always heard the myth about how military recruiters were paid to lie, so I knew that I needed to do my own fact finding prior to going to talk to one.

At the time I could not think of one single person I knew who had served in this particular branch of service. All my cousins and people that I knew were in the Army. There was no one to provide me with their personal experience which was what I needed to hear at the time. Although the internet provided great resource and information on all the service branches, at that time it lacked a face that I could relate to in order to get a feel or idea of what my own experience could possibly be like if I joined. I spent a week or so doing research so when I went into the office I was armed with the knowledge I needed to make an informed decision.

The recruiter instantly went into his rehearsed sales pitch and it was very obvious to me. The thing that he didn't know was that he didn't need to waste his time because I was already convinced that day before leaving home that I wanted to join. I allowed him to go all the way through his spiel without stopping him before I asked him any questions because I was selling him on thinking that I needed to be sold.

For mere entertainment I asked him one or two questions at the end about benefits and pay. I already knew that all branches offered the same pay and benefits but I knew that he was not aware that I knew that. He didn't exactly know how to answer the questions and he quickly began to fumble over his words. At first I thought perhaps he was new at the job because he spent more time asking the other recruiters in the office for help than he did on actually explaining things to me himself. At that moment, if I could have done so, I would have changed recruiters. I had expected to work with someone who knew what they were talking about and could provide me with direct answers.

That being stated, I was too focused on trying to get to the place I needed to be to allow this guy, or anyone else for that matter, to stand in the way of my dreams of serving my country and getting a college education. After sitting in the office and taking the practice ASVAB test, I was satisfied enough with my score that I was ready to take the real test. Later that evening I went to the Military Entry Processing Station to take the Armed Services Vocational Aptitude Battery test to determine if I mentally qualified. After I passed the test, they arranged for me to take the physical the next morning to make sure I didn't have any medical limitations that would prevent me from joining or stop me from being able to finish basic training once I got there.

To shed light on this process, you have to be mentally, morally, and physically qualified to join the armed forces. The years of the military accepting any and everyone who wanted to join, including people trying to escape jail time were long gone. The military invests a lot of money and time in training its personnel and dear old Uncle Sam likes to make sure that he is not wasting money or time on unqualified people. The government pays for the food and lodging in some fairly decent hotel for every applicant the night before they join the military and the night before they ship off to basic training for all 5 military branches. These hotels become the melting pots for young men and women to boast about their chosen branches of service, and compare who is getting the biggest perks for joining.

As the other applicants talked about all the cool stuff their recruiters had told them - like how much money they would make; all the great places to which they would get to travel; the health benefits, paid vacations etc., it dawned on me that my recruiter kind of sucked. All he wanted to know was how soon was I looking to leave to go to Recruit Training Command.

To this day, I still don't think that my recruiter was the worst person in the history of recruiting. After all, he was only doing what he was getting paid to do by getting me into the United States Navy. I do, however, think that his lack of knowledge of the product that he was trying to sell made it challenging for him to be an effective salesman.

You simply can't sell that which you do not know or in which you do not believe. In order to sell Coca Cola products, you will need to know the taste, ingredients, understand the product and the company's philosophy on that product. You have to be able to speak intelligently on a subject before others will believe that you know what you are talking about. My recruiter did not know the Navy's philosophy, nor did he know enough about the Navy's programs to pass it on to me, which could have cost him a contract that he needed.

After a few years in the service, I was recommended and selected to go on recruiting duty. This assignment had one mission and that was to recruit the best and brightest young people to join the world's strongest military. I saw this as a great opportunity for me to give back and educate young men, and women on the opportunity to serve our great nation, while achieving their personal goals.

My first stop on recruiting duty was to the Navy Recruiting Orientation Unit better known as NORU which is the official recruiting school located in Pensacola, FL. The Navy goes all out to prepare recruiters-in-training on how to find the best qualified men and women this nation has to offer to defend and represent the country. Weeks are spent studying and learning the workings of every available program that the Navy offers. This process includes learning how to identify the needs of applicants, how to overcome objections, how to work through setbacks, overcoming indifference, and reaching mutual understanding. We also had to take tests, some which required video recording, to demonstrate our level of knowledge on what we had been taught. The school made it impossible for its graduates to go into the field and fail.

There were also sales labs which required the trainees to conduct live interviews with potential applicants who could ask us anything about everything pertaining to the Navy, and we were expected to know enough about the programs to keep the applicants interested. This was a graded exercise that was videoed; we couldn't afford to get nervous, stumble over our words and fail.

It was in this environment that I was taught the art of PSS better known as Professional Selling Skills. This had to be the most phenomenal course I've ever taken in my life. Fortune 500 companies pay to send their top sales people to courses like these and here I was getting it for free. The class is designed to prepare you to become a complete and successful sales person

When PSS is applied properly during the opening, negotiation, or closing of a sale one has a much greater chance of sealing the deal than without the application of PSS strategies I now apply PSS to everything I do, and let me tell you, it still works like clockwork.

Your opening pitch should always be you; your negotiation should consist of your experience and qualifications, and your closing should be strong to drive the point home on why you are the best choice for the job or why your product or organization is the best fit for the potential client. Remember you are not the only person after the job or opportunity so you need to be the most convincing in order to obtain the north and south head motion instead of the east to west.

Putting Theory into Practice

At the conclusion of my training at NORU, I was stationed at Navy Recruiting District New Orleans. The Chief Recruiter at headquarters informed me that I was being assigned to Navy Recruiting Station Alexandria located 3 hours south of New Orleans. The station was located in a small town in central Louisiana with a low high school graduation rate and an above average crime rate which created unique challenges for any recruiter. To top it off the station had been struggling for months to make goal and the Chief Recruiter felt that it needed some new blood to bring the station back to life.

Upon my arrival to the station in July 2008, it was rather easy to see why the station was missing goal. The recruiters in the office had lost their passion to be successful at what they were doing. There was no drive or hunger; and when a man is not hungry he will not go out to hunt for his food. I came into the office starving and wanted every crumb that I saw fall from the table.

After my first week in the office, I sat down on the sofa after coming back from a long day of driving around following leads and doing blind prospecting. I noticed the two other recruiters seemed to still be sitting at their desk playing on their phones. I wasn't even assigned a goal yet so why was I working harder than those two?

My ambition was to succeed; this was the motivating factor that drove me day in and day out. It frustrated me to give my all and watch the other guys being non- productive towards the station's monthly mission. It was at that moment that I challenged them like I had never done anyone before. I dared them to be better than me. I blurted out, "I'm going to be better than the both of you, and put more people in the Navy than the two of you combined." One of the recruiters gave me a look that said it all. If looks could kill I would have been murdered that day, and maybe rightfully so.

The Recruiter in Charge was a mild-mannered guy from Texas named Chief Ragston, who sat in the back office. He looked up from what he was doing, got up, walked out of his office and told them, "That's a shame this guy just got here, he doesn't know the area or where to go and find people but he came in here ready to work but you all don't want to help him." One of the recruiters responded with a sarcastic remark by saying, "we will see how long this super recruiter attitude lasts before he is like us…but first he has to put someone in the Navy before he can make comments like that." He was absolutely right and I intended to do just that.

I hit the streets early every morning looking for people to talk to. I was willing to talk to anyone who had any interest in joining. I made phone calls in the evening to set appointments for the following day. I developed callback and follow-up lists which gave me something to strive for the following day. If or when I was not able to set or keep my established goal of appointments, I simply stayed later in the evenings than the other recruiters giving myself a fighting chance of achieving my goals the next day or the next week.

In the beginning, I even sacrificed Saturdays - which was a day off - just so I could meet with applicants and their parents to explain what the Navy had to offer. This strategy always proved to be successful because the parents appreciated being able to be a part of the recruiting process. It was easier on me also since school and work during the week meant parents weren't always available during my normal working hours.

Chief Ragston, who took notice of my ambition and began to mentor me as a rookie recruiter, which helped out very much. He provided me with the additional tools I needed to help me improve and succeed at my job. He encouraged me to keep doing what I was doing while teaching me some of the traits that made him successful as a recruiter. He shared the same frustrations that I had with the other recruiters but he refused to just give up on them and let them fail so he continued to push them even though they didn't want to be pushed.

Every December NRD New Orleans held its annual awards banquet. This was the grand finale for the recruiting district, and the command's opportunity to acknowledge the top producing recruiters for helping it with its success for the year. The Recruiting Districts do a phenomenal job at putting these symposiums together. They are well organized, as you would expect, and there are no expenses spared to show the recruiters how much they are appreciated. All 200 recruiters and countless civilian employees all come together for a day of training and celebration.

The morning was designated to the annual mandatory training which consisted of a host of speakers with a casual game or two to help lighten the mood. Once the training was complete, we would go and relax and prepare ourselves for the awards symposium scheduled for later that evening.

The symposium was a black tie event. The military personnel wore service dress uniforms that you typically see on television for things as elegant as the Commander and Chief's Ball. I can still remember it as if it was yesterday. The Commanding Officer gave out an abundance of awards and paid recognition to all of those who had gone over and beyond to help with the District's mission. I can recall sitting with Chief Ragston as several recruiters were called up and presented with awards for their outstanding service while the 4 of us from NRS Alexandria served primarily as duty clappers. We spent the entire evening clapping for others because as our station had not done enough to receive any worthy recognition. I received an award but my station finished close to the bottom that year. This made it was hard for me to be satisfied with my own individual accomplishment.

I took it all in as recruiters from the different zones teased my peers for walking away empty-handed. After the banquet, I vowed to myself and Chief Ragston that the following year would be our year to be on the receiving end of the awards while making all of our critics eat their words. I was so motivated after leaving the banquet; I was absolutely determined to give my all to make 2009 my year, even if I had the carry the weight of the station on my back.

After only a few short months into the new fiscal year, I fulfilled my promise and my hard work was beginning to pay off. Things began to turn around for our office, and people started back joining the Navy in Alexandria, La. Not only did I exceed the Recruiter in Charge's expectations for me, but I also exceeded my own. Everyone who worked in our New Orleans headquarters had taken notice of the numbers that I was putting up which was a great feeling. I was not just making the monthly quotas for the station, but I was surpassing the required new contract goal for the entire zone.

I was able to use the Professional Selling Skills that I had learned back in Pensacola on applicants, their parents, teachers, coaches etc. My success came from understanding the product and my ability to capitalize on the brand name. Plus, I was fueled with determination to succeed. I had not only become the best recruiter in my office but also out of the 5 Navy recruiting stations in my zone. Our office was doing so well that we caught the attention of the Army, Marines, and Air Force recruiters who had begun to notice the amount of traffic they saw constantly coming into our office. We gave them a run for their money every single month which helped to make the recruiting experience more enjoyable.

After only one year on recruiting, I became the recruiter of the year for my zone; I ranked #3 out of nearly 200 recruiters in my district which consisted of stations in Louisiana, Alabama, Mississippi, and Florida. I helped a station that once had the worst a reputation in the district earn its first production award in more than 5 years.

I believed that it would work and it did. My success was built off my peer's unwillingness to succeed, and failure to properly market the product. Not wanting to be selfish and take all of the glory for myself, I continued to challenge my peers to do more to contribute to the station's success. My challenges to them eventually paid off, as they began working harder. This was wonderful for me to see because it was evident that my efforts had rubbed off.

I didn't lie to applicants, or use any form of trickery to get them to sign on the dotted line. I used hard work, honesty, and my level of knowledge to close the deal. I maintained my integrity letting my name speak for itself. One's good name and integrity remained the most inexpensive form of advertisement used by the Navy to market its product.

This book isn't about my tour on recruiting. However, there is a message that I hope you take away from this story. That message is about my understanding the competition, knowing my product, how to market it, and then maximizing on the ability to close on the deal that all contributed to my overall success. Remember my initial theory was that I was going to be better than the other recruiters in my office. It was not until I was able to put theory into practice that I was proven right.

The first step in marketing yourself is knowing your product well enough to obtain buy-in from your audience. Many people make the mistake of thinking that only self-centered people spend a lot of time talking about themselves. If you are of this opinion let me share something with you. We are all guilty of this unbelievable act or perhaps sin. I don't care who you are, where you come from, what you do or where you do it, you are in some shape or form selling yourself. You may have never viewed it like this before, but yes it is true.

Who else knows your product which is self, better than you? Let me help you with the answer to this one. NOBODY! Selling is an art, not just a job. The most successful salespeople do well because they discover how to master the art of selling; to them it is more than a job. In order to be successful in selling your ideas, your needs, your ambitions, your skills, your products and services you must be completely sold on yourself.

CHAPTER 2

Confidence Sells

There is no such thing as a person without confidence. Everyone has to have confidence in something no matter what it is. Even people that identify themselves as being failures at everything…will still show a level of confidence in at least one thing. Unknowingly, they are basically acknowledging that they have a certain confidence in their failure. Truth is your confidence will never fail you or let you down. What can fail you are the things you place your confidence in that ultimately disappoint you.   After you read this chapter, it is my hope that you never look at the word the same way again.

Developing confidence in any product makes it much easier to market and sell. Confidence comes with experience. Most of us have tons of experience talking about ourselves but that does not mean we are conveying the confidence we want others to see.

Confidence is generally described as a state of being certain either that a hypothesis or prediction is correct or that a chosen course of action is the best or most effective. Self-confidence is having confidence in oneself. **Arrogance** or hubris in this comparison, is having unmerited confidence — believing something or someone is capable or correct when they are not. **Overconfidence** or **presumptuousness** is excessive belief in someone (or something) succeeding, without any regard for failure. Confidence can be a **self-fulfilling prophecy** as those without it may fail or not try because they lack it and those with it may succeed because they have it rather than because of an innate ability.

Courage is connected to confidence because confidence breeds courage. This being true, we must make sure that our self-confidence goes to work for us. The more confidence that we have in ourselves the more courage we display in taking chances. In selling and marketing ourselves to others we are displaying confidence in ourselves to talk to others about us. The objective is that they will see and buy into us as individuals and eventually build confidence in us to do business with us later. Joe Girard refers to confidence as the same as children building blocks, we find ourselves knocked down and we have to build ourselves back up all over again.

There is an old saying, "Confidence breeds confidence." If you are confident about you or something that you are trying to do, then others will also develop confidence in you, and your ideas. Most confident people are people with strong faith while less confident people exhibits fear which is the exact opposite of faith. Their minds tell them, "Go ahead, be confident, you can do it...do it now." That is the voice of faith speaking, which is the first of the two most powerful words in the entire world.

On the other hand, we all know that at times the mind is tricky and tells us, "Hold on, you just may not make it; you will fail; you can't do it, or maybe you should just do it later. That is nothing but the voice of fear trying to talk you out of taking a chance, and doing something wonderful for yourself.

It is important to understand that in building confidence in yourself there is no such thing as, "do it later. There is no reason for you to hold off on taking a chance. The greatest risk in life is to take no risk at all. There is not one successful person who did not start off by taking a chance because shooting for success is a major gamble. I have read many autobiographies of the rich and famous and in almost all of their stories it is written that they failed or did not perform well in something. Some may have failed the 1st or 2nd time around but the more they tried the more their confidence grew and the more they understood that they could and would succeed. I can guarantee you that you will fail at something… and let me tell you that it's okay as long as you get back up and keep at it until you succeed.

The steps that you take today to succeed will determine your outcome tomorrow. Decide today what you're going to be tomorrow. Get away from thinking that you will be able to start over tomorrow and become the person that you wish to be today. Today is the only day that counts because tomorrow may never come for you. You must learn to put fear and weakness out of your mind, and replace them with faith and confidence. Assume the role today of the position you look to fulfill later. There is nothing wrong or illegal about you doing this; consider it practice to prepare you for the real deal.

The reason that so many people have a difficult time telling other people who they are is because they have not fully convinced themselves of who they are or what they have to offer. You must first and foremost have faith in you so that means that you must believe in you and have confidence that you are capable of doing whatever it is that you set your mind to.

Ask yourself, "What do I mean to me?" We all know that meanings have a value to them, and things that we value carry worth to us. Learn to appraise your self- worth and don't take anything less than what you are worth. You are just what you think you are, the appraisal price that you price yourself at mentally runs over into how you speak about and carry yourself publically.

I tell myself that I'm priceless. I carry myself as such, and I speak in the same fashion. People have called me arrogant and cocky for as long as I can remember but it does not change the price at which I have listed myself at. It has nothing to do with what I say but the overall presentation of the package and in how I represent myself. Even if I kept my mouth closed there are people who would still say or that I'm cocky because of my level of confidence.

Do you realize that there is only one you? There is no one in the entire world to equal you. I don't care how many others wear the same clothes, drive the same car, ride the same bus, work at the same company, speak the same language etc., there can only be one you so you may as well get all that you are worth. You are an original in the fullest sense of the word. You are number one, and now that you know it, your job is to reinforce that fact in your conscious and subconscious mind each and every day of your life.

If, as you read this, you form the opinion that I am writing from an extremely self-centered perspective, or from enlightened self-interest, you are missing the point and the message. The message I want to convey is if you don't believe that you're the best, no one else will nor should. Present the picture that you want others to see without trying to force a brush in their hands to stroke your ego. They will speak highly of you on their own after they are convinced that you are all you paint yourself to be.

What if I told you that the most successful people in life all have the same natural power to convince themselves that they are great releasing a domino effect that makes others believe that they are? You would likely challenge me to prove my theory. I'm going to give you three examples of ordinary people with the extraordinary power to do so.

Muhammad Ali was the master at convincing others of his greatness. He told everyone who had ears that he was the best. He capitalized on every chance he was given to market himself. If a camera was on in front of him you had better believe that he was talking about himself. He was always selling himself to the public in some way. If a reporter was writing about boxing they were writing about him and what he had to say about himself. He didn't care how good his opponents were because he never backed down from his claim that he was the greatest. "I'm going to knock him down in five, he's going to take a dive." "I'm going to sting him like a bee, so he won't see me."

Ali wasn't just predicting his fights he was selling and marketing himself as the best boxer in the world. He used psychology on his opponents by selling himself as the winner going into the bout which created self-doubt in the other fighter's ability to defeat him even if they were actually a better boxer than him. He was so brilliant at it that as the referee was explaining the rules of engagement, Ali would agitate and intimidate the other fighters by staring them down and telling them how bad he was going to beat them.

Here is what I want to share you don't have to take Ali's approach to prove your greatness by telling your opponents what you are going to do to them. You don't have to do as I did and tell your co-workers that you are better at doing the job than them even if you believe that to be true. Silently convince yourself that you are better than them at what you do and they will still feel intimidated of you without you speaking a single word. Some people get it and others don't, that's just a fact of life.

President Barrack Obama sold the entire nation on this belief during the 2008 presidential election. His "Yes We Can Change," slogan was very simple but was ingenious in the message that it sent to voters. It encouraged hope and inspiration to a nation that had lost confidence in its government. It presented the possibility that yes we can change the way things are, have been, or the way things can be done. How can you not get excited or support that notion? I'm sure that the future President's advisors knew that this slogan would not just sweep the nation but it would also close the sell because everyone loves a confident person that can offer change.

The then President hopeful was not painting the image that he was great, but rather that we as a nation were great and had not yet lived up to our full potential as Americans. He gave a fresh young face to the old system of politics that young people could relate to and now demanded in big government. When the voters showed up to the polls in November we all bought into the thought of greatness so much that he was elected into office making history as the first African American President of the United States of America.

If you are still not convinced by my argument then, hopefully this last example will help clarify my point. The former Denver Bronco and New York Jets quarterback, Tim Tebow, is a natural salesman. He has never had to try hard to sell himself to the country. There is just something that lives within him that has greatness written all over it which causes others to recognize and desire to be around him.

I will never forget watching him at a 2008 press conference after the University of Florida Gators lost a game to my alma mater the University of Oklahoma Sooners putting an end to any chance of the Gators football team having an undefeated season that year. With the news cameras rolling Tim said "To the fans and everybody; Gator nation umm…I'm sorry, extremely sorry. You know we were hoping for an undefeated season; that was my goal…something that Florida has never done here. But I promise you one thing a lot of good will come out of this. You have never seen any player in the entire country play as hard as I will for the rest of the season, and you will never see someone push everybody the way I will for the rest of the season. You will never see a team play harder than we will for the rest of the season. God bless." It took less than 40 seconds for him to say those words and sell the world of sports that he was the real deal as he went on to keep his promise and lead his team to its second national championship titles in 2 years.

There is no quarterback who has played the game of college football over the last 30 years who was more popular or productive during their college career than Tim Tebow. Some may now argue that Johnny Manziel's career was just as productive but look at what Tebow accomplished compared to Manziel during his years in Gainesville, Fl. The fans loved him, his teammates admired him, his coaches respected him for his leadership on and off the field, and the nation adored him because of what he represented. He is the 2007 Heisman trophy winner, 2 time National Champion, and winner of 45 football awards during his tenure as the starting quarterback at the University of Florida and he did it all without being connected to any negative controversy or scandal.

Despite his college success, Tebow's NFL potential was much debated by the so-called football experts. NFL analyst Mel Kiper, Jr., who never played a down of college football believed Tebow did not have the intangibles to play quarterback in the National Football League. They said he was not a pocket quarterback, his ball mechanics were too awkward etc. Comments like those are enough to turn any General Manager away from selecting a player to join their football organization. His likeable personality, football intelligence and winning attitude were enough for him to successfully market himself as a good choice.

Tim was still selected #25 overall during the first round of the 2010 NFL Draft which sent shock waves through the NFL. His number 15 jersey broke NFL sales records as it quickly became the bestselling jersey in the league. No matter how many sports analyst doubted him or said that he was not a NFL prototype quarterback he continued to prove his critics wrong. He took the media by storm during the 2011 NFL season after he was named the starting quarterback in week 5 of the season for the Denver Broncos. He led the team to 8 straight wins breaking team and NFL records along the way and was even selected as an alternative to the 2012 Pro Bowl.

If you have ever listened to him in an interview or at a press conference the two things that strike you about this wonderful young man is his humility and his confidence. Tim turned his catcalls from individuals like Mel Kiper Jr. into compliments. We can't all be Muhammad Ali, President Barrack Obama, or Tim Tebow, but we can all learn to believe in ourselves and have the same winning attitude as they do. If we are going to be successful at selling and promoting ourselves, we need to police our insecurities out of our lives and adopt a winning attitude that others can appreciate in us.

. The acronym that I want you to remember is **<u>ABC</u>** which stands for acting, and being confident.

There are 3 principles of confidence that I want to empower you with:

1. People will take you at your own evaluation. Your attitudes about yourself bounce back to you from other people. If you think you have no social skills, other people will eventually agree with you. If you think you have nothing to say, you certainly will have nothing to say. If you think you're nobody then you are practically asking people to treat you that way. On the other hand,

if you think of yourself as a kind, intelligent, charming person, that's the only way you'll be perceived.

2. People will catch and mirror your emotional states. If you are enthusiastic, they will be too. If you are boring, they will also be bored when they are in your presence.

3. People tend to behave the way you think they will behave. If you think they are cold and snooty, they will probably end up acting that way to you. If you think they look down on you, ultimately they probably will. But if you think people are interesting, warm, and funny, they will not make a liar of you. If you expect for people to except you, they will.

Become the kind of person that everyone enjoys being around, a person with confidence!

CHAPTER 3

Talk your way to success

The art of marketing comes with a connection of conversing with anyone long before you arrive at whatever you hope to speak charmingly and intelligently about. The single most important element in being the kind of person everyone wants to talk with is being a person with confidence and who doesn't mind paying compliments to others.

There is a balancing act that must be mastered when dishing out either of the two. No one likes an over-confident person or someone who comes across as a "kiss up." We should always express admiration for the good work of others but only do it in moderation. On the other hand if you constantly criticize your equals or subordinates some of that criticism will rub off on you. We all know that no one likes to be around or talk to negative people, so avoid being that person. By expressing modest admiration for other's achievements, you paradoxically call attention to your own. The ability to express wonder and amazement, and seem like you mean it, is a rare and dying talent, but still greatly valued by others.

Early in his career, the French architect Jules Mansart received commissions to design minor additions to Versailles for King Louis XIV and ended up becoming Louis' favorite architect. For each design he would draw up new plans making sure they followed Louis's instruction closely. He would then present them to His Majesty. Saint- Simon described Mansart's technique in dealing with the king:

"His particular skill was to show the king plans that purposely included something imperfect about them, often dealing with gardens which were not Mansart's specialty."

The king, as Mansart expected, would put his finger exactly on the problem and propose how to solve it, at which Mansart would exclaim for all to hear that he would never have seen the problem that the king had masterfully found and solved; he would burst with admiration, confessing that next to the king he was but a lowly pupil. At the age of thirty, having used these methods time and time again, Mansart received a prestigious royal commission. Although he was less talented and experienced than a number of other French designers, he was to take charge of the enlargement of Versailles. He was the king's architect from then on.

Interpretation

As a young man, Mansart had seen how many royal craftsmen in the service of Louis XIV had lost their positions not through lack of talent but through a costly social blunder. He would not make that same mistake. Mansart always strove to make Louis feel better about himself, by feeding the king's vanity as publicity as possible because he understood that the king needed that.

The lesson that we can all take away from this is to never imagine that skill and talent are all that matters. Never spend so much time on your studies that you neglect your social skills. The greatest skill of all is the ability to make the master or person in charge look more talented than those around him.

The single most effective trait you can take into a conversation is the ability to show appreciation. In every conversation, include at least one appreciative remark. If this is something you already do you might still want to read this chapter for new techniques. According to Robert Greene, the pseudo-belief is equality— the idea that talking and acting the same way with everyone, no matter what their rank, makes you somehow a paragon of civilization— is a terrible mistake. Those below will take it as a form of condescension, which it is, and those above you will be offended, although they will never admit it. [8] Robert goes on to say that you must change your style and your way of speaking to suit each person. To truly be universally liked in talking you must be observant to your audience. Be careful to never assume that your criteria for behavior and judgment are universal.

In any conversation, business or social, what will make you stand out and be remembered later are the pleasant remarks that show your genuine pleasant side. Learn to cultivate this skill, and you will find yourself one of the best like individuals at any gathering. Some people refer to this as the ability to work a room.

Make a habit of watching for something to appreciate in other people. If you work with them, you might already know a few things to mention. If you are trying to work with them know how to mention something fascinating about the company without coming across as a kiss up because no one likes a kiss up even those with the biggest egos.

You might admire people, yet never think to tell them so. You never know how it will be received and it could leave them with formed opinions about you. You can however double your fun and effectiveness by letting people know the pleasant thoughts you have about what they may have done.

Robert Greene's book, *"The 48 Laws of Power,"* (Greene, 2000) states, "It may seem that your superiors cannot get enough flattery, but too much of even a good thing loses its value. It also stirs up suspicion among your peers." If you know a person socially, you might know enough about them to start with, "I saw your family last week, and noticed how tall your son has gotten, or "I really respect you for taking the time out to participate in the charity golf tournament last weekend."

For the people you don't know, you'll need to listen carefully to their conversation and find or make opportunities to show that you think they're a pretty fine human being. You must also become familiar with the 3 different types of conversationalist that you are certain to run into as you talk to others. Eleanor Roosevelt was quoted saying, "Great minds discuss ideas; average minds discuss things, and small minds discuss people." You will certainly discover people from each of these categories throughout life. Just try to avoid the ones who gossip more than they discuss ideas.

A gossip is someone who talks to you about others; a bore is one who talks to you completely about himself/herself; and a brilliant conversationalist is one who talks to you about yourself. The deepest principles of human nature is the craving to be appreciated. Any person that tells you that they do not care about being appreciated will prove themselves to be a liar.

The art of pleasing consist in being pleased. If you cultivate a sense of delight in the achievements of others, you have a successful career and social life ahead of you. Nothing makes people so worthy of compliments as occasionally receiving them. To put this where the goats can get it, people are more delighted in being told they are delightful.

The best way to win any crowd over is by telling them how much you appreciate them at the beginning of your presentation and at the end of it. Someone may ask why? My rebuttal would be why not? Besides the beginning and the end is what impresses people the most. Sure they will tune in to what you say in between the many other thoughts floating through their heads, but your opening and closing is all that matters in the end.

As a public speaker, one of the first things that you learn is the ability to use the podium. It gives the allusion of importance by being centered in the middle of the room. The podium does very little to add to how well the speaker will be received or how powerful they are in delivering their message. Some of the most powerful and notable speakers of today may start off standing in the center of the room or from behind the podium because they want to make sure that they have the audience attention in the beginning and in the end.

Over time the best speakers have learned that when you are able to gain and maintain your audience attention by moving around and drawing their attention to your movements the audience becomes more engaged to the message. The podium only serves as the key focal point while getting them engaged in what you are speaking about by projecting your voice at the appropriate time to keep the audience attention. It is a form of appreciation that you give back to them for being there to hear what you have to say. You want to walk into a room, comfortable in the knowledge that you are happy to be there, that you're looking forward to meeting interesting people, and can handle whatever conversational challenges come your way even in a situation like being the guest speaker.

In the past I've been asked to be the guest speaker for different functions, and although I'm always elated at the opportunity to speak, I'm equally excited that someone thinks enough of me to ask me to participate in their event. Once the invitation is accepted the speaker can't walk in and allow nerves to overwhelm them and overshadow their message. You have to walk out on the platform with complete confidence expecting to make a difference in the way that others think after your speech or presentation.

Expect to be liked and accepted. I always assume that I am liked, so if I'm liked then I must be accepted. Take for granted that people will be happy to see and talk to you. After all what's not to like about you? You were invited, you're part of this group, you're a good person so why shouldn't you be like? People will know if your attitude is defensive and insecure, or if it is relaxed and open. They might not think it through, but at some level, whatever you feel, think, and project will be picked up by others and returned to you.

Talk to win

The aim of small talk is to make people comfortable and to put them at ease. A self-conscious, tense, nervous conversationalist is going to be socially inadequate. You can't have a good conversation talking over the head of the person or making it too simple. Remember that conversations must move in a circular motion, you say something, they listen process what you have said and then they provide feedback to you while you listen and process what they say. The topic of conversation must be something that both parties are familiar with and can add a relevant viewpoint to.

Your opening meet and greet can determine how successful your entire conversation will go. Confidence starts from the moment that you extend your hand to shake someone else's. I doubt that there is a substantial amount of people reading a book like this that need lessons on how to shake hands, but in order for you to feel absolutely confident about this pre-conversational gesture, here are the rules of engagement.

- Approach the other person with hand already extended.
- Look them in the eye, smile slightly.
- Grasp hands, palm to palm, firmly but not too tightly. Try to match the grip of the other persons hand without turning it into a competition.
- While you are shaking hands, you should be looking at the other person's eyes and saying your introduction line. (for example, "I'm elated to meet you at last").
- In most areas of the United States, women and men approach handshakes in exactly the same manner. In some places women extend their hands first so that the other person knows a handshake is welcome.

Now that you have embraced with the other person and given a great introduction of yourself it is time to gain their attention through meaningful conversation.

The goal of the first few minutes of any conversation with someone you don't know is threefold: (1) to find out a few things about the other person, (2) to tell a few things about yourself, (3) to find some common ground between you and the other person. Regardless of the geographic location, in a big city or a small town, if you talk with anyone for five minutes, you will find several items in common.

The key to a good conversation is a certain back –and-forward exchange of words as I described earlier. Nothing will be more helpful to you in becoming an outstanding conversationalist than a metaphor of a tennis game. Keeping the ball in the air is an art and the point of most conversations.

Vary your contributions to the conversation by alternating among (1) making statements, (2) asking questions (3) offering a piece of information about yourself, and (4) asking something (not too personal) about the other person. An agreeable balance among these four elements will produce the best kind of conversation and give you a better chance to market yourself. Remember just because someone ask you about your family or child does not mean that they want to listen to you for 10 minutes non-stop as you highlight all of the things that are really common about kids but you think makes your child the next great rocket scientist.

To get started, you might ask the other person about their work or interest, or better yet, volunteer a little information about yourself. It is wise to keep the tone and the content of the conversation light until you find a topic that you are both interested in and want to explore at some dept. Conversational gold is found when you find a topic you are both passionate about.

Always try to use the word "you" much more often than you use the word "I." That's not to say that you shouldn't use "I" at all. In the give and take of conversation, you need to counter information offered by the other person with just the right amount of information about yourself. If you are discussing a topic, tell how it relates to you or why you're interested in it. This adds layers to the conversation and allows the conversation to continue. On the other hand, when "I" outweighs "you" in your conversation, you will notice a waning enthusiasm in the other person.

In a group, stimulate conversation as much as you can. Bring in the quiet ones in and get them involved in the conversation because they may become your biggest supporters. Pass the baton to someone who hasn't spoken; try to discover an interest common to all of you.

Look from person to person and keep a pleasant expression on your face, if your face will do that for you. If you are downhearted or discouraged, unhappy or uncomfortable, try to box the feelings up. You never want to allow your emotions to show during business social gatherings, remember don't ever let them see you sweat. Not only will you be badly out of place, but it really would blow any chance that you have to win your audience over. You want people to remain interested in what you have to say and not cause them to create reasons to avoid you.

If you are shy or self-conscious, the best cure is to approach anyone standing alone or someone who has been looking as though they'd like to talk with you but are too reserved to do so. At any gathering there is likely to be a handful of guest as uncomfortable as you are. Look for them; break the ice of your own nervousness by talking with them. Try not to spend long periods of times with any one person, even if it is more comfortable for you to do so. Social and business gatherings are not designed for two people to hole up in a corner and ignore everyone else there.

Don't worry about showing ignorance of a topic or saying "I don't know," or "No, I'm not familiar with that," or "I've never heard of such a thing." Will Rogers points out that everyone is ignorant, just on different subjects. We all undoubtedly know things that other people doesn't. And since conversations are not competitions there is no need for us to act like they are. You're not on *Jeopardy*; you will be liked for saying straight out that you don't know, and then by asking the other person to tell you more about it shows them that are still willing to learn.

Unless you are in a business discussion, avoid jargon, multisyllabic words and slang. It is important for the person that you are talking to understand what you are saying without it taking away from the professional image that you want to leave them with.

You want to establish a feeling that you're on the same wavelength. We tend to feel warm toward people who agree with us. You don't have to betray your own principles, but if you fish cleverly enough, you'll eventually pull up something you both find edible.

There is a reason it's called small talk. Anytime that you are talking with people that you don't know well, you want to skate on the surface of the ice without getting into the deep cold waters. Stay away from conversations dealing with personal philosophy, theology, religion, politics, the rules of love, or other controversial topics that may create tension.

Unless someone else starts it, and everyone in your small groups is willing to talk about it. In that case, you'll have fun and learn something along the way. You don't have to feel you have to contribute something astonishing and unique or even outrageous to the conversation. There is no rule that states that you have to be the person that always have to say something intellectual or clever. Mark Rutherford, a great musician once said, "Never try to say something remarkable. It is sure to be wrong."

The best salesperson on the sales floor is the happiest. If you hate being someplace, you can imagine your conversation will not be scintillating. So either take your happy face with you or stay at home. People only want to talk to and be around positive thinkers. Have you ever noticed how everyone avoid the negative people at work or in the family, but seek after the positive ones? Remember that a good attitude and a bad attitude are simply different ways of looking at the same situation but it's your choice.

Many of you have probably already discovered that in most conversation, you need a few "empty" words and phrases that (1) indicate to the other person you're listening attentively, or (2) encourage the other person to continue talking, or (3) fill in that expectant pause most people leave for you.

Sometimes being silent is appropriate, but it's helpful to have a handful of conversational fillers in your armamentarium. People generally don't pay close attention to these soothing little rejoinders, so it's not what you say as much as that you respond with something. Without stopping the flow of the conversation with more substantive remarks, these interjections let the other person know you're interested and involve.

Don't worry about the essential inanity of these words and phrases. Like a game score, your words provide a background for the other person's words without calling any kind of attention to them. These responses are a fairly standard part of contemporary culture, and they fill a need to give conversations the appearance of being two-sided. The problem arises when one of two things happen [1] the conversations is one-sided...we will discuss that in the next chapter, or [2] when you use the same word for everything ("Fantastic!" "Oh yeah fantastic!" "Wow, fantastic!"), at some point the expression becomes very annoying. Vary your responses and use a lowered tone so as not to call attention to your rejoinders.

You probably already use some such phrases, but you might like to collect a few new ones. Choose those that suit your personality and you can say with sincerity. To prove that you're listening, say something like:
:
"Absolutely!"
"Alright!"
"Amazing!"
"Are you serious?"
"Awesome!"
"Darn!"
"Good grief!"
"Gosh."
"Hard to believe!"

"Hmmm."
"How interesting."
"I agree."
"I didn't know that."
"I hear you."
"If you say so."
"I'll say."
"It is what it is!"
"I see."
"I see what you mean."
"Isn't that something!"
"No, really?"
"Oh?"
"Really?"
"Right."
"Right on."
"Seriously?"
"Sure!"
"That makes sense."
"That's a good point."
"Too bad!"
"Well, who knew?"
"Wow!"
"Yes indeed!"
"You bet!"
"You can say that again!"
"You can't be serious."
"You don't say! "
"You know what I mean!"

In the event that you would like to encourage the other person to continue, you should say something like:

"And?"
"And then what?"
"Continue, this is great!"

"Did they really?"
"For instance?"
"Give me an example."
"Go on."
"How interesting."
"I'd like to learn more about that."
"I hadn't thought of it that way."
"I know very little about this."
"It's hard to believe."
"Keep talking this is great information."
"Please tell me more!"
"Tell me more."
"That must have been tough on you."
"That's a very nice way of putting it."
"That's intriguing."
"That's news to me."
"What a shock."
"What do you mean by that?"
"You can say that again!"
"You mean?"

To fill in the pause that some people leave for your half of the conversation, say something like:

"Amazing."
"Fascinating!"
"Good grief!"
"Good point!"
"I agree."
"I didn't know that."
"I hear you."
"I'll say."
"I see."
"I see where you're going with this."
"Life is interesting."
"No, really?"

"Of course!"
"Oh dear."
"Oh, yes, absolutely."
"Really!"
"Right on!"
"Sure enough."
"What a deal."
"What a story."
"Wow."
"You're absolutely right."

You don't want to use the above words and phrases with someone who is delivering a monologue in your presence; it will only encourage them to continue. Instead you may want to fill that space with a subtle, polite signal that you aren't all that fascinated by what the other person is saying. Sometimes people climb on hobby horses and forget to dismount. So it is our responsible to help them down.

If you see the other person winding down his/her conversation or at least allowing you space to talk, try something like:

"Hmmm."
" I thought of you when I heard…"
"I've always wanted to ask you…"
" Say, I read an article about that the other day."
"That reminds me."

The time to stop talking is when the other person nods his head affirmatively but says nothing. This strategy may save you from a lot of wasted time. I can assure you that after a few nods accompanied by silence most people will take the hint. Be tactful, you never have to be rude to get your message across the right way. The other person is normally there as a friend, colleague, or invited guest, so you won't want to be noticeably rude.

A famous Irish writer by the name of Robert Lynd said, "A man may forgive many wrongs, but he cannot easily forgive anyone who makes it plain that his conversation is tedious."[3] In the event that the other person is riding a stampeding horse and cannot be stopped, you may be forced to use a more aggressive approach. Make sure that you throw them as many life lines as possible and hopefully they will grasp onto one before it is too late.

CHAPTER 4

Listening to Succeed

Most of us take for granted the simple verb listen, but its dictionary definition might surprise you. The *American Heritage Dictionary* says to listen means "to make an effort to hear something" and "to pay attention; heed." If you want to be a good conversationalist, remember that listening is more than simply letting the other person talk. We're asked to pay attention, to make an effort, to heed.

I know that it seems difficult at times not allowing yourself to be distracted by what is going on around you by your own thoughts while someone is talking to you. Listening is thus an active, not passive, behavior consisting of hearing, understanding, and remembering what was said that you can respond intelligently when it is your time to speak.

A good listener takes part in the conversation, offering ideas and questions to keep the flow of the conversation going. You always want to say enough to add something new, but not so much that you overshadow the other person. Good conversation is a balancing act, a teeter-totter, a turn taking endeavor. I compared it to the game of tennis in an earlier chapter, making reference to keeping it up in the air by going back and forth.

In the same way that you don't want to play conversational golf with yourself, you don't want to leave the other person hitting their own ball all the time. Listening means playing tennis, where you return the ball back across the net that was hit to you. Just like a good game of tennis, you want to see that you're well matched, and that you're both playing with the same ball.

I'm sure we all can think back over meetings, conferences, visits with friends, and other conversations and recall that a great deal of time could have been saved if everyone had listened the first time. How many times did questions have to be repeated, or answered again and again? Fact no two people processes information the same, but it does not mean that we can't all be good listeners. Perhaps I can better serve you by offering suggestion on what makes a good listener.

Here are 12 things you can do to make you a better listener:

1. You focus on the other person and their concerns.
2. You do not only listen, but you show your listening by appearing highly interested, leaning slightly forward, nodding occasionally, and saying "uh-huh" at intervals.
3. You make and maintain eye contact, occasionally breaking it so that the other person doesn't feel as though they're under a microscope.
4. You subtly mirror the other person: smile, frown, nod, and laugh when they do.
5. You ask pertinent questions that show you're following the other person's train of thought.
6. To listen effectively, you need to not only hear what the other person is saying but to understand it. This means you also ask clarifying questions. To be called a conversation, there need to be some back-and-

forwarding. Therefore, you will want to insert some of your own thoughts to the subject.

7. You repeat or summarize the other person's key points, not in a parrot like manner.

8. You should always leave a little pause after the other person's words in case they have something to add. Too many listeners take the first chance to rush into speech, which could make the conversation awkward.

9. Refer back to the things said earlier in the conversation to show that you heard what was said.

10. Be patient, if the other person searches for a word or speaks haltingly or pauses, you allow them time to complete their thoughts.

11. Try to identify with the speaker, putting yourself in their place, feeling what they're feeling. If nothing else, mentally relate the other person's experience to your own.

12. Above all, you cultivate an attitude of wanting to listen. The better you become at listening, the more clearly you'll appreciate its benefits, and you will end up wanting to listen.

The best advice that I can give a young salesperson is to learn to listen. It is also a wonderful tool to have for those who have made a career of selling. More important, it is great advice for everyone who is selling him/herself in so many ways. People from all professional backgrounds, regardless of their years of experience, degrees and credentials must be active and good listeners in order to be successful. I have listed just a few professions here to give you an example.

· Clergy
· Cooks
· Counselors
· Dentist
· Doctors
· Lawyers
· Lawmakers
· Parents
· Police
· Psychiatrist
· Politicians
· Teachers
· Recruiters

Those are just a small list of professions that demands the ability to listen. I'm sure you can come up with many others on your own. They are all in careers that require their ears pick up the smallest details in order for them to be successful at their jobs.

> *"Isn't it boring…how people always want to tell you their own stories instead of listening to yours? I suppose that's why psychiatrist are better than friends; the paid listener doesn't interrupt with his own experiences"*. — Helen Van Slyke

If you work in sales, here is something for you to consider...if you sell a product or a service you must keep in mind that what you are really selling is you. No matter how you describe the product in your hand, you are the world's number one product. During my time on recruiting all of the accolades that I received and earned came from hard work and learning everything that I could about the product. The hard work consisted of putting in long exhausting hours at the office and in the car taking people to and from the local MEPS station. Learning more about my product meant I powered up on myself more than on the organization. I needed to know who I was and what I was before I could present myself to others.

In doing so I made a wonderful discovery. I found out that if I spent more time listening than I did talking I would learn a great deal about the people that I was recruiting and also about myself as listener.

When people get comfortable talking to you it is amazing what they will disclose to you. I have learned that when I let my applicants pour out their troubles on life to me and the reason they wanted or felt they had to join the military it made it much easier for me to close the deal.

The same is true for counselors. The art of counseling is for the counselor to get to the core of the client's issue by using a strategies designed to get the client to open up about their issues. As a counselor, I have never been able to identify or assess what was wrong with my clients without them sharing with me what was bothering them. It is true that I have always been able to give informative advice to help others to improve on their areas of problems but first I must know what the problem is.

It would be dishonest for me to say that I have been able to look at them and tell what the problem was without listening to them first. Could you imagine going to a counselor, or therapist that told and they could help you with your problem without evening knowing what your individual problem was? That would be insane, and would give reason to avoid ever going back to them again.

Surveys indicate that we hear only about 50% of what is really said. How, then, can a person who wants to market himself or herself more successfully tune into the other 50 percent?

You must be willing to hear the other person completely out. People who are successful find that if they just keep listening any negative feeling others might have about them simple melts away.

We assume that because a person has two ears attached to his/her head he/she knows how to listen. I would not bet the farm on that because I would likely lose something that I've worked hard at for years. Many of us with ears are so busy thinking about what we're going to say next that what the other person is saying falls on deaf ears. The answer to the problem then is not to be thinking of what you are going to say next, but make an effort to listen attentively to the other person. There is an old saying that listening is the greater part of learning.

Listening is even covered in the Holy Bible. The Bible declares "Be swift to hear, slow to speak." Do you really think that this passage is in the Bible by mistake? God knew that men would talk more than we would listen. One of the great truths of all times is that it's hard to hear when the tongue is busy.

Good listening involves active participation on your part. No matter how long the other person is talking, at some point the law of compensation goes into effect. The other person, aware that he/she has been holding forth at some length, will pause and turn the floor back to you. This is another opportunity to market yourself, and your ideas.

Winston Churchill said:

"Speech is silver while silence is golden."

There is far more to learn by listening than there is with talking. There is a great value in silence when communicating. Silence can be healing for the soul. Silence can signify understanding when no more words are left to be spoken. Silence on your part allows you to not only hear clearly what the other is saying, but it lets you listen between the lines as well.

I know this advice may sound puzzling at first, but if you want to be heard, keep quiet. It's one of the best ways that I can tell you to be successful at marketing yourself. I just shared with you one of the most basic human fundamentals that we can make useful without thinking twice about.

After much research and spending countless hour in conversations with others while observing behavior patterns, I'm almost convinced that people that are poor listeners are not even aware that they are. The question is who is blame for poor listening habits? Only a small percentage of people with poor listening habits are rude and think that is appropriate to cut others off while they are speaking. For the larger percentage of Americans, many of us feel that it is natural to insert our point of view on the topic being discussed while the other person is still speaking.

You May Be a Poor Listener If:

1. Your attention wanders to a problem at home or work, and you lose the thread of what the other person is saying.
2. You are busy thinking of what you're going to say next, waiting for your turn to speak.
3. You rarely look the other person in the eye.
4. You can't seem to help showing that you're bored: you look at your watch, shuffle your feet, check out the rest of the room.
5. At the first opportunity, you grab the conversational ball and run with it, even if it means interrupting the other person. You'd much rather talk than listen.
6. You constantly finish the other person's sentences. This is insulting, patronizing, and irritating.
7. You really aren't interested in the other person's topic, so you change the subject.
8. You're busy judging the other person: she just said "between you and I"; "his breath sure does stink"; "he really has a horrible voice"; "he doesn't seem like the coldest beer in the refrigerator". This negative attitude is often picked up by the other person. They're not sure what's going on, but they think perhaps they won't spend much time with you.
9. If you're in an office setting you tend to multitask while conversing with someone. This way you think, as you file reports, stack up the outgoing mail, and log off your computer.
10. You are completely silent. You figure listening means shutting up, whereas the other person would appreciate hearing a word or two from you.

11. You like to one-up the other person. If they've read a good book, you've read two. If they attend a professional football game, you've got season tickets in the skybox.
12. You rush the other person, giving the impression that they are taking far too much of your time: "Yeah, you already mentioned that, so what did you have to pay finally?"

Let's face it nobody truly likes a poor listener. They are normally the people that struggle to get ahead and are passed up on promotions. In all fairness if you can't listen, then you are unlikely to be able to follow direction, or care about the needs and concerns of others. If this sounds like you, then it will by default make you a very poor leader.

As a person with years of leadership experience, there are certain things that I have learned as a leader along the way, the importance of listening has by far been the most significant one. Here is what I want to do, I want to give you a few secrets or shall we say tips for listening.

Tips to Listening Eight

1. *Keep your mouth closed* so your ears will stay open.
2. *Listen with all your senses.* Listen first with your ears. Keep them wide awake. Never settle for just 50 percent, get the whole story.
3. *Listen with your eye.* Maintain eye contact, it shows you're hanging on to every word. We've all heard the expression "in one ear and out the other." No one has ever heard, however, "in one eye and out the other."

4. *Listen with your body.* Use body language for total awareness. Sit up straight, don't slouch. Lean forward to be more attentive. You always want to present an alert appearance.

5. *Be a mirror.* Smile when the other person smiles, frown when he or she frowns, nod when the other nods.

6. *Don't interrupt.* That breaks the speaker's train of thought and just breeds irritation.

7. *Concentrate.* Pay attention to the other person at all times. This is no time to glance at your watch as if you have somewhere more important to be. This is not the moment to trim your fingernails, yawn or light a pipe.

8. *Listen between the lines.* Try to hear the "fine print." All too often what a person doesn't say turns out to be twice as important as what he or she does say. A tone of voice, an offhand expression, a shading, an embarrassed cough – all are tip offs that a person is saying something, but not in words.

There they are: eight good tips for learning to be a better listener than you were before. In doing so you are gaining a far better chance to sell and market yourself successfully.

Just think how lost you'd be if you couldn't listen. Someone once posed this question: If you had to do without one of your five senses – sight, hearing, speech, touch, and smell which one would you pick? Most people immediately say hearing. They claim that they would rather be deaf. Research suggests that is not true because we all like to hear what is going on around us.

Did you know that people adjust to being blind a lot quicker than they do to deafness? Those who are without sight seem to learn a different way to see with an inner eye and often see far more than we can imagine. Take the movie, "Ray," for example where Actor Jamie Foxx played the role of the late legendary musician Ray Charles Jr. In the movie Ray used his hand to feel the skin of a woman that he was interested in. By feeling her skin with his hand working his way up the women's arm, it revealed the weight of the women to Ray. However, being without hearing is to live in a total world of sound. Being unable to listen is a far greater burden than being unable to see.

Imagine a presidential debate is schedule to come and one of the candidates that are hoping to receive the party's nomination is a hometown local and someone which you know personally. He or she comes out and receive a standing ovation. You can see that the crowd is pumped and spectators are cheering and jumping with excitement. You are so overwhelmed with joy and spend a majority of the time on the phone with friends talking about how big the moment is that you fail to realize that the T.V. is on mute and you miss out on the amazing job that your friend did at the debate. That would be similar to what it must feel like to be deaf. Think about it. Aren't you glad you can hear and listen?

Change Your Listening Habits NOW!!!
· Add the daily listening rules to your exercise list and do them every day.
· Make sure you don't buy back the sale of yourself with your big mouth.
· Remember, the other person isn't interested in what you have to say until he's had his say.
· Write this on a three-by-five index card and put it where you can see it every day: "Often, to say nothing at all is better than saying a mouthful".

CHAPTER 5

Talking in Public

In the previous chapter we refined our listening skills, but we all know that conversing is not a one way street and it requires that after we have listened that we must also speak if we expect the conversation to continue. For those of us who have the ability to talk we need to make sure that what we say is well received and easily translated by the person or people on the listening end.

Over the last few years I couldn't help but to notice that people are no longer talking to each other. Most of us are comfortable when sending emails and text messages to express our point of views but can't say what we need or want to say in person.

Perhaps we can credit modern technology for robbing us of the ability to communicate with others face to face. It is far easier and less confrontational to speak our minds through text messages or emails, than to stand before the person that the messages are intended for and still share our thoughts.

I don't want anyone to think that I'm against texting or emailing because Heaven knows that I do my fair share of communicating from my mobile devices as it feels that I'm always on the go these days. In fact many people run their entire businesses from afar due to this wonderful technology because it is convenient and makes our life easier. You will get no argument from me. After all, why sit in an office for 8 hours if you can get the same job done by simply using an app on your mobile device to talk, send and receive emails or fax?

Conversation in public places has decreased dramatically in the last century. We can say, "well it is not safe to stand and talk to people in the streets like it once was." There may be some truth to a statement like this but I feel that because of inventions like the cell phone and host of other notebooks and gadgets that we have at our disposal to help us to communicate with each other to the point that people no longer feel that we need to stand chattering on the sidewalks or in front of stores in small downtown areas like we once did.

It very well may be because of the hurry-hurry influences of contemporary business life and the instant responses of the computer that we have grown impatient when we must stand in line. Striking up a conversation with someone might slow us down and cause us to miss the latest trending tweet or post. What if it's our turn to check out and the other person still want to talk and we are in the in the middle of providing an update on our mobile device? How would you normally handle a situation like that?

There are times when you will find yourself exchanging a few words with someone in the uncontrolled spaces between home and work: airports, airplanes, supermarkets, bookstores, Laundromat, malls, waiting rooms, bars, concert and movie lines, dog parks, resort pools, post offices etc., and you will not be able to hide behind the phone in your hand. Are you ready to step off the island of isolation and rejoin civilization where people are not afraid to talk each other?

You run into two kinds of people in public: those you know and those you don't know. Of those you know, some might be social acquaintances, others might be business connections.

Social acquaintances are easiest because you have a history, you know what to talk about, and you can have more of a personal conversation with them. With people from work, you are warmer than you are with strangers but you do not suddenly become friends simply because you've run into each other outside of work. There are plenty of people that I have worked with but didn't associate with outside of work and just because I run into them, it does not mean that suddenly I will become their BFF.

These happenstance meetings are usually too short for any meaningful exchanges. Instead, the most inane conversations are acceptable and, in fact, appropriate. It is understood that saying something bland is a way of acknowledging that the other person is a human being without, however, invading the person's privacy or wanting to become best friends in the next few minutes.

Most often, a simple exchange is the norm: "I wish I'd gotten a cart. I only meant to pick up a couple of needed items. "I do the same thing." A commiserating sigh or a shake of the head and you're finished.

At other times when you find yourself is someone's company for more than a few minutes, the conversations might be extended. However, both people must make sure the other person is interested in talking. One person wanting to talk and one person not wanting to talk doesn't make a conversation. When one statement is met with another and a question, and that is met with a statement and a question, it's likely that a casual conversation is underway.

In public, people have a natural curiosity which is why you acknowledge those around you but do not enter into a full-fledged relationship with them.

Because of changing cultural priorities-primarily the isolation brought about by long workdays, too many hours alone in a car commuting to work, and hours in front of the television- most of us are experiencing a sense of isolation. Many of us look upon others as threats to our privacy, resources, and success. For these reasons, our contacts with each other in public need to be kind, supportive, and engaging as we make them, not only as a sign of our goodwill but for our long-term well-being.

We have all heard the saying, "treat others like you want to be treated." This is ever so true when we are dealing with people in public places. Always acknowledge others with a smile and a nod, even if we are not familiar with whom they are. Common courtesy is appropriate, so you should never get confused about that which means even if you don't know the other person, you should still know how to greet them. Respond to a greeting at the same level that it was offered: "Beautiful morning." "Certainly is." Obvious today is shaping up to be a lovely day." "Absolutely, I could not agree with you more." It is important that we understand the correct amount of feedback to give in accordance to what is being said.

Have you ever wanted to talk to an attractive person on the bus or train but ended up waiting too long and letting him or her get away? Follow these steps to quickly spark a conversation the next time you're smitten, and never lose the love of your life (or at least the love of the week) again

Understand the environment. Everyone is just trying to get from point A to point B, and they may get off the bus, train, or subway at the next stop. Thus you can't hesitate if you're going to talk to someone. Keep in mind that few people actually want to talk to strangers on their trip, but some will, especially if you seem nice and interesting. Be decisive, but don't be aggressive.

Carry a prop. Bring some reading material that you can pretend to read. It will make you feel and appear more comfortable. Don't wear headphones unless you want to appear unapproachable. However you do **not** want to look like the guy in the picture. Every normal person will probably run away and scream.

Scope out the situation. OK, so someone has caught your eye. Before you try to initiate a conversation, make sure they're not with their significant other. If they're with anyone at all, proceed with caution, but remember, their companion may just be a friend or relative, or he or she may be a complete stranger who has the same idea that you do.

Position yourself for success. If you see the person while at the bus stop or train station, wait until he or she gets on the bus or train before trying to converse. Follow them in discreetly and sit opposite them if possible. You'll have a good chance to make eye contact this way, and besides, you might appear somewhat invasive if you sit down next to them. If they're standing, stand near enough to them to be able to speak with them, but don't get too close for comfort

Try to make eye contact. Making brief eye contact can show the person that you're interested and help you gauge whether he or she is interested in you. Glance at the person (don't stare) and try to hold their gaze for just a second or two. Don't look away before she does! This shows confidence. Try to make eye contact again after about 30 seconds. If the person makes eye contact with you again, they probably find you attractive. Don't be too obvious, but make sure the person can see that you're looking at them. If they can't see you, you can't expect them to make eye contact.

Smile when making eye contact the second time. A small, but genuine smile makes you appear interested, friendly, and approachable. If the other person smiles back, you're probably in luck.

Use appropriate body language. Don't cross your arms or turn away from the person. Make yourself appear open and comfortable, and exhibit good (but not freakishly good) posture. Don't look at your watch or a clock constantly, as it will give the impression that you are in a hurry and the person might not talk to you, because they don't want to bother you.

Read the person's body language. If he or she exhibits open body language toward you, that's a great sign. If the person turns away or buries his or her head in a book, that's not so good.

Ask the person a question. A question is a great way to start a conversation, but not just any question will do. Ask an open-ended question that requires more than a "yes" or "no" answer. For example, ask, "How do you get to the Eiffel Tower?" instead of "Does this bus stop at the Eiffel Tower?" What you ask isn't really important, as long as it's not invasive, insulting or insane, e.g., the Eiffel Tower questions might seem dumb in New York.

Keep conversing. Listen attentively to the person's response to your question and then just make small talk. If the person is interested in you, the conversation will probably flow fairly naturally (unless he or she is shy) and you may be able to get a phone number or email address. Then casually be the first to leave. This will establish a self confidence in both of your minds. If the person isn't interested, you'll probably be able to tell pretty quickly.

These are all simple tips that will help you to talk and communicate with others in public places including on public transportation.

- If the person is sitting and you're standing, position yourself so that your crotch isn't in the person's face.

- When making eye contact, keep your facial expression light and friendly, rather than straight and serious.

- It can take some courage to actually talk to a stranger on the bus or train, but remember that this is really an ideal situation. If the person isn't interested, you probably won't see them again, and even if you do, you can just sit far away from them.

- If a person hunches over or turns away from you, or if he or she fails to make good eye contact, they're probably not interested, but not necessarily so. Some people are just shy, and public transportation tends to accentuate this shyness. Don't expect much from a person who shows negative body language toward you, but at the same time don't assume he or she is not interested. If you're particularly brave, take a chance.

- Get help from a friend. If you have friend, bring him on the train/subway/bus with you. Sit near the person you want to talk to, and start talking about something interesting or surprising. If you notice the person looking over or listening, smile and include them in the conversation by asking them what they think.

- If the person makes eye contact and displays positive body language, but you can't get up the nerve to talk to him or her or you have to get off at the next stop, write down your phone number or email address on a piece of paper (a newspaper will work), smile at the person as you get off the bus or train, and hand them the piece of paper. If the person calls or sends you a note, great. If not, no big deal. Keep in mind that this is a very low-percentage approach, so don't expect a call. If you have time, it's best to just muster the courage to talk to the person.

- Look for a ring. Look to see if your potential paramour is wearing a wedding or (if they're a woman) an engagement ring. If they're wearing a ring (ring finger of left hand) they're off limits. If they wanted you to approach them, they would have left their ring at home on the dresser.

- If you get shot down and feel embarrassed, just get off at the next stop and board the next bus or train. Maybe someone else will catch your eye. If so, try again. Even if someone might be interested in you in other situations, they might not feel like talking on their commute, or they might be preoccupied. Don't take rejection personally.

- If you have a friend, bring him/her on the bus with you and talk about some interesting or surprising things that has happened or something about you such as "Guess what! I did..." Something that grabs the person's attention and might make them comment and from there you could converse with your friend the person. With a friend you might feel more comfortable. If the person talks with his/her friend a lot maybe you can figure out what the person is interested in, if he/she has pets and then you could talk about such things and they might join in.

- You can gesture to the woman you're attracted to who is wearing headphones and signal her to take them off. Then proceed with normal interaction. If she is interested, she'll keep them off.

CHAPTER 6

Creating Your Steps to Success

What if I told you that there is a 3-step program that can dictate how successful you can be in life, would you believe it? Someone reading this would tell me that there is no way that a 3 step program can or would ever make you successful. As cliché as all this may sound, there are actually real benefits from using these formulas with steps.

You have likely heard of or may have participated in 3 steps, 5 steps, 10 steps, and even 12 steps programs in the past. Some of them may have been great tools while others were probably busts and did not benefit you in any kind of way. If you don't retain anything else from this chapter, remember this: 1. Set a goal, 2. Make a plan, and 3. Make it happen! This is the only 3 step program that you are in full control of at all times.

There is an old saying "if you fail to plan, then you have planned to fail." Many of you reading this book may have been alive long enough to know that this is a very accurate statement. Besides the very few individuals who are born into royalty, life is not carved out for us. We have to go out and carve a place out in this world for ourselves. Today is your day of redemption. If you are one of the millions of people who feel that you spend your life running on a treadmill trying to keep up with the current level without moving at all then this chapter may just be for you.

There are only two kinds of people in life, there are those that make things happen for them and there are those who let things happen to them. This is often referred to as either being proactive or reactive. Proactive thinkers are always planning and thinking outside the box, they plan for almost every aspect of life and everything that they involve themselves in. On the other hand reactive thinkers just seem to go with the flow and react after something has already taken place.

Let's look at Sean Combs, Mark Zuckerberg, Steve Jobs, Dr. Dre, Donald Trump, and Russell Simmons. They are the people who began planning at an early age. They set certain goals for their lives and where they wanted to be by a specific age so they developed plans on what they needed to do to get there on schedule. It is safe to say that these individuals are all proactive because they planned to succeed and they did. Proactive thinking people are often the hardest working individuals in class or on the job. They are very business savvy, and they are observant, paying attention to everything that matters from the stock exchange, political races, housing market, etc. They are your goal setters with a purpose.

Although Donald was the son of a wealthy of New York City real-estate developer Fred Trump, he still had to work his way up in the company. He was 1 of 5 of his father's children and knew that his father's success did not belong to him. In his book, (Trump, 2004)"*The Art of the Deal,* he discussed his early life decision to work for his father. [4]

"After I graduated from the New York Military Academy in 1964, I flirted with briefly with the idea of attending film school...but in the end I decided real estate was a much better business. I began by attending Fordham University...but after two years, I decided that as long as I had to be in college, I might as well test myself against the best. I applied to the Wharton School at the University of Pennsylvania and I got in...I was also very glad to get finished. I immediately moved home and went to work full time with my father."

In 1971 Trump moved to Manhattan, where he became convinced of the economic opportunity in the city, specifically large building projects in the Manhattan area. [5] Trump began by landing the rights to develop the old Penn Central yards on the west side, then with the help of a 40 year tax abatement by the financially strained New York City government, which was eager to give tax commission in exchange for exchange for investments at a time of financial crisis. He turned the bankrupt Commodore Hotel into a new Grand Hyatt [6] and created The Trump Organization. [7] Trump claimed that he was practically broke this gave birth to his plan to acquire and develop the old Penn Central for $60 million with no money down. His goals, plans, and hard work helped him achieve a net worth of $3.9 billion, as of 2014. He set a goal, made a plan, and made it happen, this is just what each of us must do if we expect to succeed like Donald and others have done.

Set realistic and attainable goals for your life. There is no such thing as setting the bar too high, but it is always a tragedy to set it too low. What if I told you that most people are under achievers by default, would you believe me? They either don't plan properly or they surround themselves with people who are content with the cards that life has dealt them and they fail to set any kind of goals that will actually challenge them to push themselves. Success starts and ends with preparation which equates to planning. Remember this: people who plan have far less problems than the people that have a problem with planning.

I discovered the winning formula to my marketing plan years ago as I decided to jump off of the programmed mechanic device of life and began to march to the beat of my own drums. My formula and marketing plan works great for me, but it may not come as natural to others so here is an outline of how you can develop your own plan.

There are many advantages of having a plan. First of all, it will encourage a long-term view of your mission or organization. It will stimulate thinking to make better use of your available resources. From an internal perspective, the plan will serve as a vehicle to achieve consensus and buy-in which will foster unification of efforts. Overall, a good marketing plan will focus on your strengths and will help prevent repetition of past mistakes. What exactly is a Marketing Plan?

"There are three kinds of people.
Those that make things happen.
Those that watch things happen.
Those that wonder what happened."

My only question to you is which one are you?

By definition a marketing plan is a written document that spells out the goals, strategies and tactics to gain and/or maintain a competitive position, as well as the results sought. A good marketing plan is really a living document (and should be treated as such) that defines the action your business needs to take in order to achieve certain goals. A good plan should align with your goals and define how you will reach your target audience

So, how do you get started? There are a variety of ways to begin, below are key tips that you may find useful in developing your successful roadmap.

Tip 1: Conduct an Overall Assessment
First, you should do an assessment of your current marketing materials. Look at what is working and what is not working. Determine how effective your marketing efforts have been and what kind of results were generated. You also need to look at how your clients perceive you. The way you see your company may be very different from the way your audience views your company.

Tip 2: Set Your Goals
As with any initiative or task, there has to be a goal in mind. Without a goal, how can you measure your success? The goals should also align with your company objectives and should be specific, obtainable and measurable. You need to have a plan that is substantial enough to show a return on your investment, but it also needs to be flexible enough to evolve.

Tip 3: Determine Your Target Audience
In order for your plan to work it is critical that you know who your audience is so that you can determine the best way to reach them. You need to know as much about your target audience as possible.

Tip 4: Perform Research

Good research can go a long way. It is the backbone in how you determine and improve your strategy. Research is concrete feedback and without knowing these facts, you would be guessing about which steps to take next. This can cause you to miss your target audience all together which will lead to missed sales and opportunities. Research can be done through a variety of ways that may include focus groups, surveys and the internet.

Tip 5: Determine Your Strategy

Your strategy is your "logic" through which the goals and objectives that you have established will be achieved. The strategy will outline how a particular product or service will be promoted to your target audience. Marketing strategies are used to increase sales, drive brand awareness, launch new products and generally provide profit for a company.

Tip 6: Define Your Tactics, Budget and Resources

Now you are ready to take the plan to the next level in which you determine the appropriate tactics to utilize in order to meet your goals. When you choose the tactics, summarize what it is, how to implement, why you should use it and what you expect from the outcome. Also, determine how you will track and measure each tactic: what gets measured gets results. You also need to determine who will implement the tactics. Can the implementation be done in-house, or will you need to look to outside sources?

Tip 7: Evaluate Your Plan

You spent a lot of time creating your marketing plan and you also need to include ways to know if your plan is working. You'll need to give your plan time to work however. Some things will need to evolve and some things will need time to ramp up. Keep this in mind when evaluating if something is working or not.

These are key elements to consider when you are developing a plan. It should be built with an end result in mind and fit the specific markets you are reaching. It should also be flexible in order to meet the needs of your audience, because as we all know in today's world, things can change quite rapidly. Your plan should be simple and easy to understand. It may look great on paper, but if no one can comprehend the plan, then it will simply find a home on the shelf and collect dust. In order to grow a strong company, you must have a strong marketing plan

CHAPTER 7

The Benefit of Developing Others

Until this point, I've talked to you about knowing your product, confidence sell, talk your way to success, listening to succeed, creating your steps to success, etc., as a means of helping you to become the most marketable person in the room. Now I want to talk to you about building others through leadership and influence.

This chapter won't make you the greatest leader in history once you finish it but it will provide you with something that all good leaders already know which is to always take care of your people. True leaders always produce new leaders. I'm a firm believer that when you get to the next level in your life or career, you have to create ways to give back to develop others. I have been in a leadership role for a great number of years now and what I have come to understand is the single most important thing that I can do on any given day in my office or out in the field is to nurture the development of my people.

The truth is, either we are born natural leaders or we are not, for those that are gifted with the trait of leadership the task comes easy and they stick out everywhere they go. For those who were not born with the trait, it takes work to help them to learn how to lead. Positions and titles do not make any of us leaders it only gives us an advantage on the organizational chart of where we work. Sure you may have the title or rank to be called a leader but that does not guarantee that you are leading anyone. If you are ever in doubt just stop look back and see who is actually following you.

When people are truly following your lead, they are emulating your style and upholding your standards regardless if you are around or not. So I ask, are you a leader in your home, family, on your job, or in your community? If you said yes, you should have no problem with developing others to become the kind of leader that you are.

Over the course of my career I observed many great men and women whose presence demanded attention as soon as they entered into a room, they opened their mouths to speak and people hung on to their every word as they were able to win everyone over. It was not because they required anyone to respect them but because they understood the power of buy-in. Let me explain; buy-in is the acceptance of and willingness to actively support and participate in something (such as a proposed new plan or policy).

It is necessary for all leaders to have buy-in with their people. You can attempt to be an authoritarian and rule with an iron fist but that will not get you far. People will take more pride in completing a task or supporting a change once they feel that they were included in the decision making process. There will be times that you may have to make quick decisions without gaining the acceptance of your people and that is just fine.

Can everyone be a leader? Yes, but does everyone want to be a leader? No. I'm well aware that everyone can't be or won't want the responsibility of leading and developing others. It should however at least be a tool that we all attempt to use to pull the leader in others out. Here is a little known fact about leading:

There are 3 groups of people when it comes to leading others:

The first group, are natural leaders and can get anyone to follow them anywhere. They have vision, are charismatic and are universally respected. They are always willing to lead because they were born to do so.

The second group, are people who want to be leaders but lack the basic fundamentals to inspire people to actually follow them. They typically complain about everything that those who are willing to lead do.

The third group, are people who have no desire to lead, will go along with the flow without complaint, and pay attention to everything that the other two groups do. They often are the keepers of useful information.

Good leaders will find a way to motivate the third group, develop the second group, and coach the first group of people so that they can reach their full potential as leaders. Regardless of which group that the people around you belong to, it is your responsibility to build them up to be the best that they can be. You must learn the behavior of individuals, so you influence their behavior through manipulate without them knowing it. Everyone has something that motivates them and it is your job to figure out what motivate your people.

There are literally thousands of people that I've helped to influence in some kind of way. I made it a priority to learn as much about them as possible so I could better understand their behaviors and know what to expect from them. The more that you know about your people the easier it becomes to lead, influence, and develop them. I enjoy identifying leadership characteristics in others and helping to develop them as leaders. I've made it a professional goal to teach individuals who are hungry for knowledge, teachable, and willing to step forward how they could eventually put me out of job.

If that last statement strikes you as being odd then perhaps this chapter will serve you well. It's an old term that you hear from those who are or that have been in leadership positions. All it means is to develop the people around you to do the same job that you are doing and they will perform accordingly whether you are around or not. Teach them the ins-and outs of what your job and responsibilities are so that you won't be the only person capable of doing it. This will help you in more ways than one because it will allow you to put your attention and efforts into other areas.

Any knowledge that goes unshared is useless knowledge in my opinion. What do we have to gain by keeping knowledge that can help others to ourselves? Now let me ask you what do others have to gain through us sharing knowledge that they need? I'm sure that we can all answer these questions with ease but many of us don't do it with ease.

My style of leadership may not work for you, and yours may not work for me but there are plenty of leadership styles for us all to choose from and incorporate as leaders. Let's take a closer look at what they are and how these styles can benefit us.

The 3 leadership styles all successful leaders use!!

All successful leaders, from Eisenhower to Patton, understood the three primary leadership styles. They all knew how to use them, and when to use them.

The three primary leadership style are; participative, delegation and authoritarian.

- **Participative** - is where you allow your subordinates to have a say in what happens. This works well, in promoting a sense of team, and helping give confidence in your employees that you value their opinion. Of course while you do ask for their input, you reserve the right of final decision for yourself.

- **Delegation** - is where you delegate or put someone else in charge of a particular project or task. This instills confidence in that employee, and allows them to learn how to be a leader themselves.
- **Authoritarian** - this is the simplest. You make the decisions, it's your way or the highway, end of discussion.

Most leaders tend to fit into one of the styles above. Now for the big revelation: a good leader uses all three approaches, depending on the situation. A successful leader does it all.

If those that I am leading fail in any kind of way I take it as a blow to my leadership but when they flourish I rejoice in silence, allowing them to enjoy their own accomplishments. Leaders should always take responsibility for the failures of their team but allow the entire team to be given credit when the team succeeds.

If you travel around the "how-to-succeed-in-business" lecture circuit enough you end up hearing a lot of interesting stuff about competitive strategy, disruptive technologies, resource allocation, asset management, and the like.

Interesting—and sort of beside the point. Because when it's all said and done, winning teams win because they have the best players and a coach who knows how to make the sum greater than the parts.

It's as simple and as complicated as that. Simple, because as soon as people hear that dictum, they typically mutter, "Oh, yeah." It's hardly a controversial notion that great players plus a great coach equal great performance. Complicated, though, because actually doing it is very hard. We get distracted. The board wants a presentation, or a customer is getting pesky. Or we lose our nerve. Or we get tired. Whatever. Something, anything, makes us forget that winning is about leading your people. And about leading them in four very specific ways.

FIRST, the leaders of winning teams always — always — let their people know where they stand.

We're not talking about "Good job, Robert," or "Thanks for your hard work, Tom." Effective leaders let their people know whether they are star performers without whom the organization would writhe in agony or whether they should be thinking seriously about finding another job.

Amazingly — to me, at least — the habit of continuously evaluating each team member is a rare and wondrous thing. Sure, leaders evaluate their people all the time — but they too seldom share those observations with the team members themselves. In the silence, stars become disaffected and leave seeking more appreciation, either in the soul or the wallet, or both. Meanwhile, the solid center wanders around in undirected ignorance, and the real underperformers drive their teammates crazy because others must carry their load (and no one upstairs ever seems to do anything about it).

By contrast, on winning teams, leaders spend the vast majority of their time lavishing love on top performers. Yes, love: rewarding them for every contribution, building their self-confidence so they have the guts to take on even greater challenges, and holding them up as a role model for others on the team. Similarly, on winning teams, leaders devote a lot of energy to middling performers, relentlessly coaching. And as for the do-nothings, leaders present these individuals with a sense of reality, spending only the time necessary to help them put together a résumé and find a job where they will be more successful.

Unfortunately, in most organizations, managers spend an inordinate amount of time working around their worst people, counseling their aggrieved co-workers and rearranging work to accommodate their incompetence. They also spend a lot of hours fretting over how they can possibly break it to their underperformers that they're terrible at their jobs without hurting their feelings. It's all backward. Rather than hurting their feelings, you're doing your underperformers a favor if you let them know they need to go, and the sooner the better, before they have to look for work in a recession. After all, who were the first employees to be cut in 2008 or 2009? You guessed it: mainly those who should have been set out on new paths years earlier.

SECOND, winning teams know the game plan.

There's never been a Super Bowl team that charged the field thinking, "We'll figure this out as it goes along and see what happens". And there will never be a winning business team that lacks a clear sense of how the competition thinks and fights—and how it's going to think and fight better. Nor has there ever been a winning team that didn't believe that winning would make life much, much better in very real ways.

Don't get me wrong. I am not a huge fan of strategic planning as it is commonly taught in business school, nor as it is practiced in every company. Lengthy reports about strategy from headquarters or consultants—in particular, those that involve PowerPoint slides—frankly makes me nervous. They usually claim to predict the future in a way that no one can anymore. No, in today's global market, strategy means picking a general direction and executing like our lives depend on it. And that's what winning teams do.

Here's the catch. Most leaders explain the game plan in mushy, vague terms. "We need to gain market share. That's going to mean beating out our competition," they might say. "Everybody's quota is going to be doubled, and we're reorganizing so that everyone is reporting to someone new". "Change is hard, but it's necessary".

Ready, forward — what?

On winning teams, leaders infuse their people with crazy-positive enthusiasm about what winning will look like for the company and, more importantly (as it's often forgotten), for them as individuals. "Look, Groovie Smoothie's killing us," they might say. "Their on-time delivering makes us look like we're driving horses and buggies around here. But we can beat them by coming up with a better idea for efficiency every single day. And when that happens, your life is going to change and everything is going to get better. Our company will start to grow again; we can open more shops, you'll have more job security and a chance for advancement. Even though we're going to enter into a long, hard slog of change ahead, at the other end of it you'll be smarter, richer, and your life will be more exciting."

THIRD, winning teams are honest.

Or let me be more precise. On every single winning team, you will discover that the leader is candid; you must be completely transparent as a good leader. Oh, sure, there are exceptions. But in time, they always backfire. Because when people don't say what they mean, play politics, or withhold their ideas, everything gets screwed up. Resentments accumulate. Cliques form. Good people leave. Work slows down.

By contrast, the simple truth is that candor breeds trust. And when a team is infused with trust, people play to their better angels. They share ideas freely. They help their colleagues when they're stuck and need an insight. What they do every day then becomes about the group's success, not their own. They're not worried about not getting the credit for some big win; they know a teammate will say something like, "Hey, don't thank me. Marcus was the one with the "eureka" moment that set the whole thing in motion." And Marcus will say, "Thanks. I may have had the idea, but you guys executed."

The candor-trust connection has another benefit: it promotes an environment of risk-taking. Who wants to try something new if they sense they'll get a stick in the eye (or worse) should they fail? Leaders of winning teams encourage their people to take on huge challenges and let them know that they're safe no matter what happens. And then they make good on their word.

Only in such environments will people be bold. And only bold teams win.

FOURTH, and finally, winning teams celebrate.

No idea I talk about gives people hives more than this one. Maybe it has something to do with the recession—"How can you party in times of austerity?"—but people balked even before the economy went south.

Most leaders don't understand the tight link between celebrating small successes along the way and achieving the big one at the end. But it's irrefutable. Teams that get pizza when they land a new client, or go on trips when they hit a sales milestone, or otherwise whoop it up every time something good happens create a delicious dynamic. They teach people what it feels like to win, which is, well, a very good feeling. It makes people want to win more. In fact, they never want the feeling to go away. So they do everything to keep winning.

We would call it magic, except there's nothing mysterious about it. Like all four of our maxims here, the only mystery about winning teams, really, is why there aren't more of them around.

Remember, the more you develop others the more you are also developed as a leader!

The End!

 About the author

Cornelius Jones is passionate in his desire to meet the needs of others. Towards that end he works to help people find the strength they need to move forward in life. Drawing from his own life experiences, Cornelius believes that with the correct tools and teaching anyone can transform their own life.

"The Power of Marketing You," marks his 6th book since 2010. He is an internationally recognized leadership expert, speaker and author who continues to soar to new heights in his career as a writer.

Also by Cornelius D. Jones

Living Out of Order and Without Favor

Changing the Man Within

Don't Call Me Black, Call Me American

Inspirational Being

Building a Beautiful Relationship

Notes: